Creative Photography

Creative Photography

Aaron Scharf

Studio Vista: London

Reinhold Publishing Corporation: New York

A Studio Vista/Reinhold Art Paperback edited by John Lewis
© Aaron Scharf 1965
Set in 10/13 Garamond
Published in London by Studio Vista Limited
Blue Star House, Highgate Hill, London N19
and in New York by Reinhold Publishing Corporation
430 Park Avenue, New York
Library of Congress Catalog Card Number 65-13370
Printed in the Netherlands
by N.V. Drukkerij Koch & Knuttel, Gouda

Acknowledgements

To the following authors and their books: Franz Roh, *foto-auge* and *L. Moholy-Nagy, 60 Fotos* for illustrations on pages 57, 63, 64, 68, 69, 70, 74, 66, 77. To Laszlo Moholy-Nagy, *malerei, fotografie, film* for illustrations on pages 55, 58, 59, 67.

To Louis Chéronnet, *Petit Musée de la Curiosité Photographique* for the frontispiece formerly in the Sirot collection and to Georgiana Houghton, *Chronicles of Spirit Photography* for illustrations on pages 32 and 33. To Walter Woodbury, *Photographic Amusements* for illustrations on pages 24, 34, 45 and 52 and to Frank Fraprie and Florence O'Connor, *Photographic Amusements* for illustrations on pages 25 and 79.

To H. P. Robinson, *Art Photography* for illustrations on pages 18 and 19 and to MM Demachy and Puyo, *Les Procédés d'Art en Photographie* for illustrations on pages 26, 28 and 29.

To Joshua Taylor, *Futurism* on page 39 and Sr Carrieri, *Futurism* on page 41 and 75. To Pierre Mac-Orlan, *Atget. Photographe de Paris* on page 47.

To Georges Hugnet, *La septième face du dé* on page 76. To Andreas Feininger, *New Paths in Photography* for illustrations on pages 80 and 81 and to Marcel Natkin, D.Sc., *Fascinating Fakes in Photography* for illustrations on page 83.

To those artists, collectors, galleries and publishers who have kindly allowed their works to be reproduced. To the Principal, St Martin's School of Art, for permission to use the photograph on page 91.

The author is grateful to the Royal Photographic Society for permission to use their facilities and wishes to thank their librarian, Miss Fiona Ross, for her kind help. To Gerry Jones and Peter Jones the author is indebted for their generous help with photographs. Thanks are also due to my editors for their patience and assistance. Above all, a special note of gratitude to Marina Betts for reading the script and for her many thoughtful suggestions.

Recomposed Delacroix photograph by author 1962

Throughout the history of photography, no less than in that of the other arts, some people have believed that the medium should not be extended into areas which might obscure the identity of its original means. There have also been others whose interests and talents, whose temperaments, allowed no such respect for the medium; no calculated limitations and no fixed horizon of creativity. With the growing technical efficacy of their medium, photographers found that the camera and the various printing out stages could be more readily manipulated – this word is used for its precise meaning – and many of them employed (some of their colleagues would have said 'resorted to') whatever means were at their disposal to achieve the desired results. The more purist-minded deplored any photographic jiggery-pokery, and on a shifting scale of values dependent on the prevailing fashion opposed all new-fangled techniques while often himself employing means which had been new and equally opposed in the preceding generation.

In the nineteenth century, photographers who considered themselves artists with cameras, as others were with brushes, often attempted to demonstrate that their medium was not entirely mechanical but that it could be made responsive to the spirit as well as to the hand of the operator. Some preferred and even insisted that all the creative organization be confined to the pre-exposure stage: that the selection and composition of the subject, the lighting, focus and other controllable means be prepared for the picture-taking mechanism itself. Some believed that it was justifiable if even the post-exposure techniques of developing and printing were made sub-

Painted photograph, nineteenth-century
Courtesy Bibliothèque Nationale, Paris

ject to a variety of retouching and other procedures so long as the resulting picture would thereby be enhanced.

In 1861, for example, Alfred Wall, who was both painter and photographer, wrote a useful little book with the rather descriptive title: *A manual of artistic colouring as applied to photographs: a practical guide to artists and photographers containing clear, simple, and complete instructions for colouring photographs on glass, paper, ivory, and canvas, with crayon, powder, oil or water colours* . . . This book was produced of course before natural colour photography had been perfected. From the very birth of photography, first made public in 1839, it was generally agreed that a serious short-coming of the medium, a factor which hindered its consideration as a Fine Art, was its incapacity to record nature's colours. If the artist-photographer were to imbue his medium with as much as possible of what was available to the painter, colour became a major consideration. Despite this prevalent attitude Wall anticipated certain criticisms which his book would invite. It is no more illegitimate, he states, to paint upon a good photograph than was the practice of Leonardo, Raphael, Titian and Rubens, and numerous other eminent masters, who painted upon the abozzo, that is, upon their monochromatic preparatory sketch. He berates the paper-stainers whose 'gaudy inartistic colouring, and crude raw and hard style have brought the art into no little disrepute'. The artist, continues Wall, rejects coloured photographs because they are not paintings; the photographers sneer at them because they are not photographs. But why, he asks, 'should an art which combines the truth of the one with the loveliness of the other be thus unsparingly denounced? The best interests of photography are served by advocating its union with art.' The *manual of artistic colouring* describes techniques for glazing onto photographs, for scumbling, impasting, and for handling: imparting an appropriate surface texture to each object according to its own special nature. Consistent with the general artistic prescriptions in England at that time, Wall's recommendations about impasting were careful to prohibit the exaggerated protuberance of the pigmented surface and though the usefulness of the palette knife was suggested, any undue communication of the presence of paint was to be avoided.

But while the painter was able to reconstruct his images, to alter them in a seemingly infinite number of ways, the more imaginative photographer before the end of the nineteenth century found direct procedures difficult and on the whole unsatisfactory. The resources of pigments and brushes open to the painter were not equally available to photographers, that is if a photographic character were to be preserved in the picture; often the photograph became simply a base for overpainting in oils. Consequently, in order to endow his art with the range of subjective control possible in the more directly manipulative arts, the creative photographer had little recourse but to make his *tools*, more than his hands, capable of conveying his personal style. It is principally for this reason, I believe, that in the nineteenth century the inventiveness of photographers, in respect of their equipment and materials, far exceeded that of painters. But constantly harassed by colleagues who considered unethical any immoderate (and the meaning of that word was constantly alterable) tampering with the lenticular image, the photographer who did so was often obliged to disparage his discoveries by treating the results of his experiments as photographic prestidigitation: as camera tricks, camera magic and as so-called photographic pleasures.

A very distinguished photographer, Antoine Claudet, working from 1839 in London where he opened one of the first daguerreotype establishments, proposed in 1866 a new means of creating 'harmony and artistic effect in photographic por-

Painted photograph, nineteenth-century
Courtesy Bibliothèque Nationale, Paris

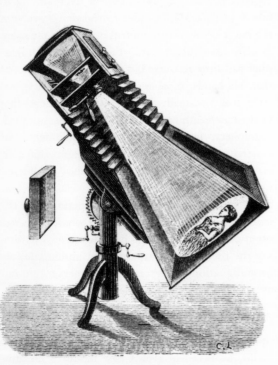

traits'. This consisted essentially of a technique of changing the focus by a lens tube during the exposure, so that at once more definition and a consistent softness of contour could be distributed throughout the various planes of the face. Addressing the London Photographic Society, Claudet recalled another process which he had employed earlier using prisms in taking daguerreotype portraits and which he again recommended in taking photographs on paper: 'It occurred to me that a certain degree of softness might be obtained by placing before the lens a square block of thick glass, or before the plate in the camera some pieces of ground glass of various degrees of fineness, for the purpose of effecting the same deviation in the course of the refracted rays forming the image, and this causing a harmonious effect.'

Like Wall, Claudet was not unaware that his proposals, or for that matter any proposals of similar nature (as innocuous as they might seem to us), would be met with derision. What does the name given to it matter, he argued, so long as the result is good? If such photographic heresies will improve a work of art is it not ridiculous to condemn them as dodges? To illustrate the effectiveness of such unconventional means Claudet described the discovery of one of the great technical modifications of steam engines. A naughty boy whose job it was to open and shut a valve during the action of the machine wanted instead to go and play with his comrades. Thinking of a way in which his absence would not be noticed he attached a cord to another moving part of the machine which did for him the work of opening and shutting the valve. The method revolutionized steam engineering. And would painters and sculptors, continued Claudet, reject any means of improving their work? Would a painter refuse to prepare his canvas with a medium which would enhance the brilliancy or durability of his colours? Is it beneath the dignity of the sculptor to

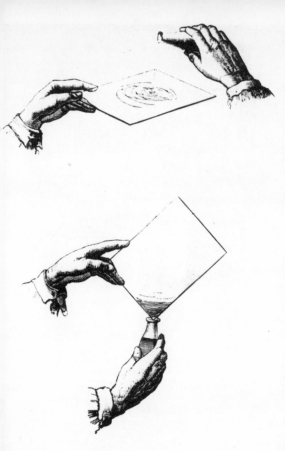

transfer to the marble the proportions of his model by means of a pantograph or some other mechanical contrivance? These words 'dodge' and 'heresy' convey no reasonable arguments. Let us then without prejudice, concludes the photographer, employ every means possible, examine any new theories or processes which are offered by thoughtful and conscientious men in the hope that we can find in them something good.

Another photographic dodge, in effect not too dissimilar to that of Claudet, had been suggested as early as 1853, in one of the very first issues of the *Photographic Journal* in London. Complaining of the pre-Raphaelite superfluity which described, quite indiscriminately, and with wearisome uniformity, every single object in sight, a correspondent praised the value of ambiguity in certain areas alternating with clarity in others, and noted that the vague tonal masses will often leave the imagination to fill up deficiencies. He therefore proposed to have images put out of focus, not by the manipulation of the lens but by the deliberate use of faulty lenses; his own experience, he stated, would seem to show that inferior optical means, combined with some of the more sensitive chemical processes, will produce good effects in this way. By using a glass that is partially streaked, some of the sharpness of the image is destroyed. What was suggested, it seems, was a means of producing differential focussing in the same plane, a factor contradictory to the physical properties of the efficient lens and today a feature often to be found, and greatly augmented, in the paintings, for example, of Larry Rivers and Francis Bacon.

A few years after Claudet's pronouncements the phrase 'diffusion of focus' had assumed some importance in the terminology of artistic photography. The suppression of excessive optical sharpness in any one plane to prevent it becoming obtrusive was now more widely recognized as essential to good

Charles Nègre: *Street Merchant, Paris* Calotype *c* 1853
Courtesy André Jammes, Paris

photography. In 1868 a description appeared of a new lens which, by means of a sliding pin projecting from a slit in its mounting, could be made to produce the *defect* of spherical aberration, counteracting the efficiency of the camera and eliminating the undesirable sharpness. It seems that many years previously Fox Talbot (the inventor of one of the first photographic methods) had suggested a means to obtain the desired effect by interposing one or more sheets of paper between the negative and the sensitive paper. In fact Talbot's calotype method itself, in which the paper negative was made translucent by oiling or waxing, was often employed by photographers in preference to that of the daguerreotype because of the soft chiaroscuro effects obtainable through the interceding texture of the paper. Even after 1851, when new negative on glass processes were known, artists like Charles Nègre deliberately used the calotype – by then already a somewhat antiquated method – in order, it seems, to exploit the opaline luminosity characteristic of that technique.

The subject of retouching in the history of photography has always been a sensitive one. Had retouching been confined to the elimination of accidental blemishes on the negative or to the most tentative spotting of light in a few appropriate places, the furor raised over 'touching' (as it was called) could hardly have been so loud or so prolonged. But can we blame the photographer who with a brush in his hand was quite naturally moved to embellish the plate: to heighten, or soften, the contrasts, to add a few obliterated details, to furnish an appropriate background setting and otherwise turn the mechanically obtained image into a work of art. There must have been a strong compulsion to do so. What the abolitionists of retouching disliked, quite understandably on their part, and what they so often decried, was the great extent to which the original image had been tampered with. Examples abound in portrait photography in which creative touching has been instrumental in transforming some very tarnished physiognomies to pristine condition. The new Fountain of Youth was all the more effective since it was generally agreed that the photograph could not lie and thus were many missing virtues miraculously restored. The doctoring up of early portrait photographs, not least the application by hand of colour, has produced what to us are some of the most delightfully abominable hybrids in the whole history of portraiture – but which to the connoisseur of the last century must have seemed nothing short of execrable.

When in the 1850s, for the purpose of furthering their art, the first photographic societies were formed, the regulations governing photographs admitted to their exhibitions rigidly prohibited the inclusion of any which had been coloured by hand or had in other ways noticeably been retouched. A few irate letters of 1856 will be sufficient to indicate both the extensiveness of retouching and the temperature of those who valued photographic purity. One, aggressively signed 'A Photographer', insisted that the photographic society in London exclude all retouched photographs – coloured ones particularly – from their exhibitions because any obliteration of photographic character would be injurious to the profession: the introduction of *touched* pictures is objectionable. Nothing need be added to a good photograph. This practice has been carried to such an extreme that many pictures are now nothing but touches. Another correspondent asked that works exhibited by the society should be required to stand on their intrinsic merits, on the positive result of photography alone. Retouching had reached such proportions, it seems, that it became difficult to find photographs which had not in some way been embellished by hand. This evil procedure, the writer complained, should be banned and such photographs ought to be exhibited with paintings where

they belong.

The views of professional retouchers were elaborately set out in a book on the subject by a M. Bech (Paris 1888). This art, he wrote, despite the opposition of critics scandalized to see a natural work modified by artificial means, is used today universally, as a necessary complement of photography. Criticisms made on the basis of heavy-handed examples of the retouching art rather than on those executed with more finesse are to be deplored. The critics of retouching are no more justified than if one condemned photography itself after having seen a few bad examples. A good retoucher should be able to work over the whole of the image without either impairing the resemblance to nature or allowing the means to be seen. Later Bech describes in absurd detail how to do so. He based his work on the conviction that, however perfect in subject or quality, every negative needed to be retouched. An artist not only should rectify what had escaped the lens but might additionally improve upon nature: what is so unusual than that one should exceed a little the limits of one's model, in a discreet manner? If one has a portrait made by an artist in pencil or charcoal, this artist will not produce something resembling an untouched photograph, but a picture just like a good photographic negative modified by a good retoucher. The artist will make a work of art and if the resemblance is reasonably successful nothing will be said. Is it then because the one is made by a single means only, and because the other is the result of two methods of apparently contrary nature that the whole art of retouching is criticized? Though perhaps M. Bech's indignation is somewhat exaggerated (his protests are considerably more extensive than the extracts referred to here) he nevertheless touched some sensitive spots relevant to the great aesthetic arguments debated in Paris at exactly that time. It was then generally held that nature could and should indeed be modified in the production of representational images; the academicians Meissonier and Bouguereau as well as van Gogh and Gauguin all concurred in that. Here their differences were determined only by questions of degree.

Obviously then, many photographic artists found themselves in an ambiguous position, for their works were excluded not only from the exhibitions sponsored by photographic societies but from those of paintings as well. An amusing account is described in 1861 in which a photograph, coloured by hand, was inadvertently admitted to the Royal Academy exhibition that year and even hung on the line. But most photographs of this kind, despite their similarity with certain styles prevalent in painting, would not so easily escape detection. Though it is impossible to estimate how many pictures – equal mixtures of photography and painting – were then produced, the paucity of their surviving numbers is perhaps largely accounted for by the official interdictions placed upon them.

In 1859 Alfred Wall made the significant observation that the growing facility with which photographs could be taken was the cause of its decline as an art. Most photographs produced, he said, were lacking in any artful qualities. Photographers had not set high enough standards for themselves, depending more on the mechanism of their equipment than on an appreciation and study of pictorial art. While the education of the art student, he concluded, was long and arduous just to obtain an elementary knowledge of his profession, that of the photographer amounted to little more than the necessary technical instruction with which to produce sharp, clean, well exposed and well developed pictures. That to the photographer seemed the legitimate end of all his efforts. The literature of photography amply demonstrated its devotion to mechanism: to cameras, to lenses and baths; to processes and modifications of processes; to a multitude of trivial improvements. Though the mechanism of any art is of great importance it should, Wall stated, be considered *the means* and not *the end*.

At just that time, the photographer Henry Peach Robinson published a paper describing his 'combination printing' method – *On Printing Photographic Pictures from several Negatives*. Ever conscious of the artistic potential in photography, Robinson compared his combination technique with that of the artists of ancient Greece. Zeuxis, he maintained, painted his famous picture of Helena from five of the most beautiful girls the town of Crotona could produce. He united the most perfect features of each in one single figure. And in that same manner our Victorian Apelles conceived his pictures. His first combination photograph, 'Fading Away', was printed from five negatives and we may estimate the seriousness of this artist when he informs us that in its fabrication the principal figure had three years' practice in expression for photography before a satisfactory picture was taken. So scrupulous was Robinson in the construction of his subjects that in his 'Ophelia' the figure itself, consistent with the philosophy of the ancients, was composed of two different persons; the head was taken from one model, and the figure from another. In a later publication, *Pictorial Effect in Photography* (1869), Robinson described his combination printing method in detail. To enable the photographer to control all the formal elements in his picture the use of special cloud negatives, of toning and stopping out varnishes, of leather dabbers, cotton wool, curved pieces of zinc or cardboard, or prepared vignetting glass and the use of the finger was recommended. Though fundamentally it was desirable that all the component parts of a combination print be unified in one homogeneous image this was exceedingly difficult, perhaps impossible, to

H. P. Robinson: *Nor' Easter*. Three stages in combination printing, *c* 1890s

accomplish. For not only did all the inconsistencies of scale, focus and tone, of light source, betray the composite origin of the work – though today this might be looked upon as a virtue rather than a vice – but more subtly, for example, the luminous aureoles which usually attend dark objects against lighter backgrounds were lacking and suggested the dislocation of forms from their contexts.

In 1889 new methods for the transformation (the distortion) of photographic images were proposed by the well-known inventor of an early natural-colour photographic process, Jacques Ducos du Hauron. About fifteen years earlier an Italian photographer had obtained similar images using cylindrical mirrors to produce photographic caricatures. But du Hauron's *Photographie Transformiste* effected by the use of movable slits in place of a lens was ultimately of a more serious nature when applied to art. Just as this method can make the model appear ridiculous and ugly, says du Hauron, 'so, if one wishes, can it correct and embellish it. Thus in the case of a photograph or, better still, in the work of

Photographic *Transformations* by du Hauron and others *c* 1889

an artist who has little regard for the rules of aesthetics – where for instance a face may be too squat – a judiciously calculated setting of the two slitted sections will produce harmonious proportions, giving the picture a grace and nobility lacking in the original.'

Employing a not too dissimilar procedure, the landscape photographer Roland Briant in 1894 made photographs through a slit in a card in place of a lens. The resulting images, as in his 'White Robe of Winter', bear a curious resemblance to Cézanne's landscape paintings of the same period. The manner in which objects are segmented into rectilinear patches conveying the sense of a high degree of control is alien to ordinary photography and is closer in form to that found in certain post-Impressionist paintings.

The means devised for the distortion of photographic images are considerable in number and proliferate from about the time of du Hauron's new method. The possibility of photographing from a variety of reflecting surfaces which themselves distort the subject is immediately obvious. But other, more elaborate, processes to effect what was sometimes called Photo-anamorphosis involved for example the use of conically-formed negatives and, in printing, exposures made on obliquely tilted paper. Even a very delicate procedure in which the negative emulsion itself is lifted from its support and 'reconstituted' has been suggested.

Many photographers in the 1880s and '90s felt it imperative that they depart from the unimaginative and purely mechanical manipulation of the camera. One writer in *Studio* (1894) with good reason declared that throughout the world photography as exemplified by its leading practitioners had become hopelessly stereotyped and utterly mechanical in its approach. We may add to this the incontrovertible fact that in painting too – as a glance into the illustrated salon and academy exhibition catalogues of

Roland Briant:
The White Robe of Winter 1894 *Studio*

the period would sufficiently corroborate – a state
of appalling stagnation had been reached. It can
hardly be only by chance that this awakening of the
creative spirit in the ranks of the photographers
coincided with that of the various post-Impression
ist movements forming in Europe. They believed
just as painters like Redon, Gauguin and van Gogh
believed, that they must not be bound by any system
which proposed the supremacy of optical logic
that they should alter and if necessary distort natural
appearances; that they could produce visual lies and
thus come closer to other kinds of truths. Typically
the *Studio* article was called, 'On some methods of
suppression and modification in Pictorial Photo
graphy' and its author, as did others before and after
deliberated on the question of degree; how far one
could go in the artistic reassessment of natural
forms. It had become obvious, he noted, that the

Cézanne: *Mont Sainte-Victoire c* 1904–06
Philadelphia Museum of Art, George W. Elkins Collection

tendency in pictorial photography was to increase the subjective appearance of its pictures to communicate the individuality of the artist. He advances the startling idea that every graphic representation produced by the action of light on sensitive grounds, with or without a lens, with or without a camera, is necessarily a photograph. But startled by his own audacity he makes the proviso that no 'absolutely new matter' should be added to the photograph.

Not surprisingly, the most imaginative uses of the photographic process were described in books which humbly confined their often brilliant ideas to the lower artistic strata of parlour pastimes and manipulatory magic. However, the authors of *Les Récréations Photographiques*, MM. Bergeret and Drouin (1893), stated prophetically that there should be no loss of dignity when serious artists or scientists learn and create from recreational activities. Their

A 'Conical Portrait' 1890s

book included a wide variety of photographic techniques and suggestions for making unusual images, among them the recording of perpendicular aerial views, the patterns caused by magnetic fields and light trajectories, all of which were later to be of special significance in the work of Moholy-Nagy at the Bauhaus.

At the end of the century we find an excellent example of the mentality of the photographic artist in the writings of Alfred Maskell and Robert Demachy whose new application of the older but little-known gum-bichromate process promised to revolutionize artistic photography. For however much freedom was allowed earlier in the selection and arrangement of the subject and in the adjustments of the camera and lens, and whatever was condoned in the retouching of negatives, the greatest reservations had been made in respect of the embellishment of the finished product – the photographic print itself. Intrinsically, the gum method postulated the manipulation of the photograph, for not only was the print made on a photo-sensitized surface pigmented at the discretion of the artist, but in washing away the unexposed portions of the image a wide range of sprays and other techniques could be used to obtain the desired effect. Gum prints more closely resembled pastel and charcoal drawings than they did photographs. They could simulate other graphic processes, and were sometimes referred to as photo-aquatints.

When they were first exhibited, exclamations of delight with their un-photographic character elevated them to categories usually reserved for artists working with the pencil and brush. Though so-called *papier velours* or *artique* papers coated with bichromated gelatine were on sale commercially, many photographers utilizing that method prepared their own. A saturated solution of bichromate of potash in gelatine into which some pigment was

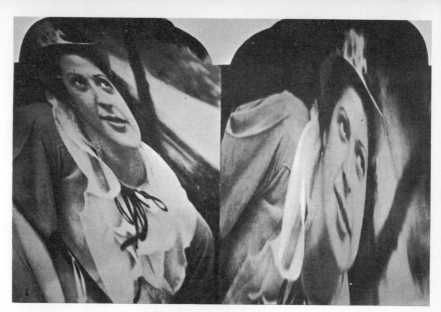

Campana-Bandranas:
Distortions by printing on inclined paper *c* 1937
Permission Amphoto, New York

introduced was used to coat the printing surface, textured drawing papers and often even canvas being employed. Those parts exposed to light hardened according to the degree of illumination, the rest were either utilized in some effective manner or dissolved away. The permutations of this medium (never yet fully exploited) are prodigious. The picture, in relief, can be built up gradually on any kind of base; superimposed images are obtainable by adding new layers of bichromated gelatine; multiple colours can be applied in one or successive layers and inking and brushing techniques of almost unlimited variations are possible. Soon after Maskell and Demachy proposed their method the Japanese showed themselves very adept in the photographic use of powdered metallic colours with which they produced, it was claimed, some very unusual gum prints. To illustrate the adaptability of the gum-bichromate process I cannot refrain from describing the gruesome suggestion which was offered in 1896 for 'post-mortem' photographs. These were to be made by using the ashes of some cremated

R. le Bègue: *Sketch*. Gum print *c* 1906

loved one, applied to an earlier photograph in the following manner: 'they will adhere to the parts unexposed to light, and a portrait is obtained composed entirely of the person it represents'.

The two photographers discussed the current ethic concerning retouching which sharply distinguished between the negative and the print. Whatever was condoned in the retouching of negatives, no such liberty of modification was allowed in the case of prints. Despite the concessions made to photographic manipulation it was still prescribed that only light acting chemically through the negative should be responsible for the final result. No alterations of the print, no hand work, was permissible. Possibly such prohibitive attitudes were to some extent due to the sudden appearance of that radically new technique. Previously, the probability of altering by some photographic means the deposit on the printed surface had been rather remote and the most advanced arguments against decorum in creative photography centered around the treatment of the negative. It is also clear that at that moment at the end of the century when the arts were undergoing such rapid changes photographers could not remain unaffected. Methods and practices, Maskell and Demachy noted, which were proscribed but a short time before, were then not only tolerated but encouraged. The advocates of pure photography were undoubtedly shocked and displeased but they could not preclude the inevitable. A premium had been placed on individuality as opposed to mechanism in art. The expression of personality rather than the formulation of a common, mechanistic style had become an aesthetic imperative. As a pictorial process pure photography was no longer satisfactory. The art-loving public, they believed, neither knew nor cared how the photograph was produced. Only the result counted. But conservatism often lurks in the hearts of radicals and these

Hugo Henneberg:
Old Square at Kempten
Gum print *c* 1906

two advocates of the gum-bichromate method, as had the writer in *Studio*, qualified their remarks, consistent with the general mentality of the *avant-garde* artists of the time, by disapproving of certain techniques, particularly that involving the addition of any absolutely new matter to the print. This, we shall later see, had a special importance in the art of the twentieth century. Enumerating a number of practices then almost universally countenanced in the manipulation of photographic negatives, Maskell and Demachy finally demanded to know whether a photograph was to be produced solely by mechanism or whether it might be modified by the skill and application of the artist.

Contemporary with Maskell and Demachy was one of the most cantankerous and vociferous ad-

Hugo Henneberg: *Old Square at Kempten*
Detail, gum print *c* 1906

vocates of pure photography in the whole of the nineteenth century. Categorically opposed to retouching of any kind or to any other means of altering the photograph after it had been taken was P. H. Emerson, for a time the fiery and influential proponent of photographic naturalism: 'Retouching is the process by which a good, bad, or indifferent photograph is converted into a bad drawing or painting.' Emerson entirely rejected the gum-bichromate method and the claims that it gave individuality to the photograph. Mere verbal juggling, he snorted. As for its results: 'We have examined what are given out to be the best examples of this work and find them almost false in tone and bad in texture, and in no way whatever comparable to a naturalistic platinotype, say. Every good quality of photography is

lost in them except the mere outline of things, the weakest part of photography . . . The process merely uses photography as a basis for after "hand-work" of a most fumbling or bungling description.'

One however suspects that all this had a deeper meaning, for at that time it was increasingly apparent (just before photography in natural colours was perfected) that the camera was likely to equal or even supersede painting as a recorder of natural conditions. Perhaps because of this Emerson and others of like mind did not want to see photography's new estate squandered on the vagaries of extra-aesthetic embellishments. Proposing a naturalism more radical even than that of the Impressionists he proscribed anything other than the direct execution of photographs in their entirety before nature, denouncing all dark room hocus-pocus. Photographs would not require retouching (he stormed) if in the first place they had been taken correctly. Though now this line of reasoning may appear rather extreme, it was in the nineteenth century an understandable one. Most artists then considered as essential the homogeneity of all pictorial elements: the photographic logic (which had become optical logic) of transition in tone and space. Even the works of artists like Gauguin, van Gogh and Cézanne, in which photo-optics are superseded by the demands of the inner vision, are nevertheless still of the nineteenth century in their structural uniformity. It is inconceivable that a serious painter or photographer would then dare to propose the deliberate juxtaposition of heterogeneous forms and techniques – much less materials – in a single work of art as was later done in the twentieth century. Perhaps it was also the kind of ambiguity produced by the hybridization of photography and the more manual effects intrinsic in the gum process, the aesthetic miscegenation of the impersonal with the hand-made, which Emerson found so repugnant.

Furthermore Emerson was entirely against the idea of equating photography with art. And though he conceded that a number of alterable elements were at the disposal of the imaginative photographer: selection of view, lens, focus, exposure and method of printing, photography, he insisted, could never equal painting in its ability to produce personal statements. It was still a mechanical process, subject, despite its manipulative latitude, to the limitations of the machine (*Naturalistic Photography*, 3rd ed. London 1899). Emerson did not say this out of humility for he was far from being a humble man. It was only, he claimed, that he hated pretentiousness and imposture. Yet his book may as well have served painters as photographers for many things relevant to both are there discussed, including a potted history of art from the Egyptians and Assyrians to James McNeill Whistler (whom he greatly admired) with gratuitous notations on the optical theories of the famous Helmholtz and Rood.

Undoubtedly the most potent force attributable to photography is the credibility of its images. Yet the truthfulness of its image is an arguable point. Theoretically, under strictly administered laboratory conditions consistently uniform recordings of natural objects might be taken and we should then have one definable type of image of the physical world which we would agree was objective. But in practice no such conditions prevail. Instead, all the mechanical and chemical idiosyncrasies of the different photographic media, and all the vagaries of human application attend photographic production. Thus it is difficult if not impossible to arrive at a single criterion for an absolutely true photographic image of nature. The important thing is that despite the many different ways in which photographs record nature there is an almost universal belief in their truthfulness. We have learned to see nature more or less as the average camera 'sees' nature. It

Spirit photographs *c* 1881

is this widespread and profoundly conditioned acceptance of photography's generic image as true which makes it so incalculably powerful in the pictorial arts; a factor as meaningful to artists who are concerned with the reproduction, as to those concerned with the reconstitution of the physical world.

In this respect a most intriguing event occurred in England in 1863. It was then widely believed that, like the camera, the human retina on the point of death retained the last image which was registered upon it. In the case of murder by assault its promise for crime detection was obvious if only the

tiny picture on the iris could be extracted and enlarged. Thus, within thirty hours after the violent demise of such a subject in England, an experiment was made by a photographer, one Mr Adams. *The Photographic Times* reported the event: 'There was a great deal of dust flying and a great crowd collected, which materially interfered with the success of the experiment; but notwithstanding these unfavourable circumstances, Mr Adams succeeded in taking a tolerably fair "negative" ... He had taken an ambrotype picture of the eye of the deceased, and then rubbed out everything but a single object apparently in the centre of the eye; this was placed under an ordinary magnifying glass. At the first glance the object appeared blurred and indistinct, but on getting the proper focus the outlines of a human face were at once distinguishable.' So exaggerated then was the efficacy of the all-seeing mechanical eye and so readily was its recorded image acceptable that those present had no difficulty in seeing the details of the face of the murderer. They saw what they wanted to see: long nose, prominent cheek bones, black moustache and other sinister distinguishing features.

Photography was believed capable of recording even supernatural phenomena. Throughout the latter half of the nineteenth century we read of séances and experiments in which, under certain conditions, the spirits of dead persons materialize on the innumerable photo-sensitive plates prepared by the credulous and the unscrupulous alike. Huysmans writes in *Là-bas* of the experiments in photographing 'visible and tangible spectres' undertaken by a certain Dr Crookes, these being very important to the satanists of the day as confirmation of the possibility of casting spells. In 1882 Georgiana Houghton, a spiritualist, published her book, *Chronicles of the Photographs of Spiritual Beings and Phenomena Invisible to the Material Eye*. The pages bristle with letters and testimonials corroborating

Prof. Bowditch: Composite portrait of twelve Boston physicians *c* 1887

the genuineness of spirit photography. Not only do recently deceased loved ones, departed household pets and remote ancestral configurations appear in such photographs, but so also do the photogenic ectoplasms of the Saviour, saints and of a host of unidentifiable and menacing ghostly emanations. 'On the third negative to our great delight appeared a tall figure in long white garments, whom we both instantly recognized as Mamma' (from Mr Hudson's photographic studio, 1870s). There was a 'faint manifestation on another plate of a circlet and cross above my head'. Miss Houghton, it must be noted, was well aware that, though many were genuine, a large number of counterfeit spirit photographs were being manufactured.

In spirit photography we may have the first effective, if not artful, use of multiple-exposed and superimposed images. Quite naturally the authors of those amusing books on photographic pastimes included instructions for producing these spectral forms. Several methods were described to summon forth the pictorial apparitions. The obvious one of judiciously double-exposing the plate, the second time in the presence of the assembled victims, was

Muybridge: Consecutive series photograph from *Animal Locomotion* 1885–87

E. J. Marey: Chronophotograph of English boxer,
probably 1880s *Permission Cinémathèque Française*

often employed. So also was that of utilizing the
actinic rays from a background screen painted with
fluorescent quinine. This image was first rendered
invisible by exposure to sunlight and later, with the
unsuspecting subject discreetly posed before it
recorded on a photographic plate.

Perhaps a reference should be made here to another use in photography of superimposed images
purported to be 'scientific' in character. Photo-

graphy had served well the study of physiognomics, particularly after about 1860 when the ephemeral moods of the human face could be registered with all the accuracy afforded by the instantaneous camera, Darwin's *Expression of the Emotions in Man and Animals* (1872) being probably the most distinguished example. The passion for discovering generic types in each category of human society gave rise to the composite portrait photograph. Portraits taken of a dozen or so representatives of some occupational or otherwise classifiable group, notwithstanding the fact that usually their individual physical characteristics were exceedingly diverse and that the whole system was fallacious, would be combined by superimposition and the 'type' discovered.

The attitude that superimposed images may have a positive value in pictorial representation begins in the history of modern art, probably in the 1880s. The appearance in photography of these forms was immediately preceded and stimulated by the large series of consecutive motion studies first taken in the '70s by Eadweard Muybridge using a battery of successively exposed cameras. Though the resulting images describing the phases of locomotion in a number of human and animal activities were produced both for artists and physiologists interested in the correct positions of their subjects in any single moment of time, they may as whole series have suggested to artists on the search for modern pictorial means a new way of representing movement. Degas' use of cinematic progressions quite likely bears some relation to early *carte-de-visite* photographs taken in series and to those made later by Muybridge. As in the photographs his compositions often appear to be of a single figure momentarily fixed in several consecutive phases of movement. For the purposes of scientific study in the physiology of movement Muybridge's photographs were of limited value and a more accurate technique for

E. J. Marey: Chronophotograph *c* 1890 *Permission Cinématèque Française*

Boccioni: Study for *Dynamism of a Cyclist* 1913
Courtesy Raccolta delle Stampe Achille Bertarelli, Milan

taking sequential images was devised by the American artist Thomas Eakins, and in France about 1882, by the distinguished physiologist Etienne Jules Marey. Eakins and Marey photographed from each viewpoint with only one camera, the successive representations of a moving figure being recorded on a single plate. Because the intervals between exposures were in duration only a fraction of a second most of them were inevitably superimposed, stretched out in a kind of expanded accordion of time. The kinetic signs thus produced – oscillation patterns, the sharp edges of momentarily fixed appendages blurred off in the direction of movement, the strange trajectories described by moving parts – could not but influence, especially after the '80s, artists whose concern was with the representation of motion.

As can be expected, the most overt use of the characteristic features of the chronophotograph – as it was called by Marey – and of similar images

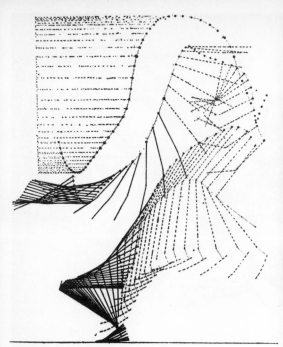

E. J. Marey: Diagram of a jumping figure. From a chronophotograph, *c* 1885

Duchamp: *Nude Descending a Staircase, No. 2 1912 Permission Philadelphia Museum of Art, the Louise and Walter Arensberg Collection*

sometimes discovered in earlier photographs is to be found in the work of cartoonists and illustrators, in the more popular arts in which aesthetic convention is not such an intimidating force. But apart from what appears to be a rather tentative use of chrono-photographic form in the work of Seurat, in paint-ing generally it does not appear until the naturalistic tradition is totally superseded in the work of the Cubists and the Futurists. It is difficult to know to

A. G. Bragaglia: *The Slap c* 1913
Courtesy Il Milione, Milan.

what extent Picasso and Braque were influenced,
if at all, by stroboscopic photographs like
Marey's or by cinematic idiosyncrasies – literally
the 'flicks' – in the infancy of that medium. We
are almost certain, however, that Marcel Duchamp, the creator of the infamous 'Nude Descending a Staircase' (1912) and the Futurist artists Balla
and Boccioni particularly, found in photographs by
Marey and his followers some of the visual means
for their representations of the dynamism of modern
life. Perhaps one of the first photographers to see
a positive aesthetic virtue in the multiple exposure
and superimposition of form – apart, of course,
from the spirit photographers – was Anton Giulio

Bragaglia, an associate in Milan of the Futurists. As early as 1913 he effected images in motion by multiple exposure in which a stratification of both fixed and blurred objects produces a vivid sensation of kinetic energy suddenly released. Consistent with the wild and enthusiastic declarations made in the many manifestos of the Futurist artists and poets Bragaglia proclaimed the concept of Photodynamics. Typical of that aesthetically headstrong period he played with potent, canonical sounding words like Photomovementistics and Photocinematographics. But his aim was clearly stated: 'We wish to bring about a revolution in order that photography may make progress and may be purified, ennobled and elevated to the level of art.' Bragaglia believed that this could only be possible if 'static realism' and its commonplace records of fixed moments of time were rigidly excluded from the art of photography

Photographers were of course as influenced by painters as were painters by photographers, and practically every movement of note in painting was paralleled by similar developments in photography As it became increasingly clear that many painters were deserting or relinquishing (as the case may be) the traditionally ascribed role of anecdotal art and with it the photographically descriptive style photographers willingly and often joyously filled the vacancies. 'It is well that they should study the character and direction of the coming change with a view to their own interests', advised one spokesman for photography in *Photograms* (London 1916) But it was also obvious to the same writer that however great photography's triumph, the more spirited or perhaps restless, among them could not be satisfied with what they believed were merely superficial recordings of life. Inspired by the many new antinaturalist movements in art which proliferated from about 1907 with the appearance of Cubism, they too would venture into the realm of the unseeable -

Alvin Langdon Coburn: *A Vortograph c* 1917 *Courtesy the artist*

their subject not Life but Art.

The future of pictorial photography, according to Alvin Coburn, writing an article of this title in the same issue of *Photograms*, must be one in which the photographer was alive to the spirit of the time. 'Why should not the camera also throw off the shackles of conventional representation and attempt something fresh and untried? Why should not its subtle rapidity be utilized to study movement? Why not repeated successive exposures of an object in motion?' Under the influence of the Cubist, Max Weber, Coburn supported the scandalous idea of an exhibition of abstract photography. And most significantly, everyone now has a Brownie, he declared, 'and a photograph is as common as a box of matches'.

The possibilities of the camera had not yet begun to be realized, said Coburn; the beauty of design displayed by the microscope seemed to him a wonderful field to explore from the purely pictorial point of view. And of a very different order of photographs he suggested that 'the use of prisms for the splitting of images into segments has been very slightly experimented with, and multiple exposures on the same plate have been neglected almost entirely'. Coburn obviously wanted to produce a photographic counterpart to Cubism or one of its derivatives like Vorticism which was then raging in London. Coburn's contribution to the next issue of *Photograms*, entitled simply: 'A Vortograph', was the only one of its kind in the whole album which otherwise was filled with the usual range of rather tiresome, not to say trivial, pictorial subjects.

Coburn, who wanted so much to do things 'stranger and more fascinating than the most fantastic dreams', made very little impact with his Vortograph and his critics did not even do him the honour of treating it seriously: 'A very entertaining half hour' (went one facetious comment) 'might be spent

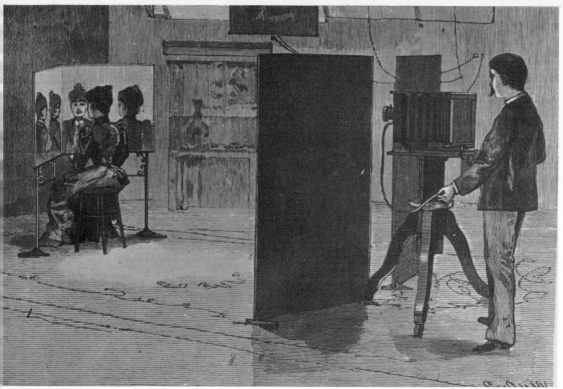

Multiphotography c 1896

H. L. Bostwick: 'Multiphotograph' of Cissy Fitzgerald *c* 1896

in finding out which way up Alvin Langdon Coburn's "A Vortograph" looks best.' The diaphanous crystalline appearance of Vortographs was produced by the use of mirrors which multiplied the image of whatever object was used and, more important, transformed that object so that it was no longer identifiable.

Now the technique of mirroring was by no means new when Coburn adapted it to his Vortographs. As a photographic amusement it had for some time been given the pedestrian designation 'multiphotography'. We find, for example, in a well-known book on novel effects obtainable with the camera, *Photographic Amusements* by Walter Woodbury (1896), a useful description of this process: 'Multiphotography which was at one time quite popular consisted in posing the sitter with his back to the camera . . . In front of him are arranged two mirrors, set at the desired angle to each other, their inner edges touching . . . When an exposure is made and the negative developed, we not only have the back view of the sitter but the full reflected images in profile, and three-quarters positions as well . . For photographing articles where it is of advantage to secure a number of different views of the same object this method of photographing with mirrors opens up quite a wide field of possibilities'. This idea of simultaneously representing several view points of an object in one picture was later to play a central part in the theories of Cubism and Futurism. Related to such forms are photographs of Parisian shop windows and their surreal reflections executed about forty or fifty years ago by Jean Eugène Atget who found these images in nature rather than fabricating them by superimposition or by the use of mirrors.

Photographs taken without a camera were not new with the appearance in the early 1920s of so-called Photograms. Fundamentally, they are at least as old

Eugène Atget: Reflections in a shop window, Paris early 1900s
Courtesy Henri Jonquières, Paris. Collection Berenice Abbott

Fox Talbot:
Photogenic drawing 1839
Courtesy André Jammes, Paris

as photography itself, for it is probable that almost
a half-century before the discovery of photography
was announced by Daguerre in France and Talbot
in England in 1839, photographs by a direct contact
method had been produced by Tom Wedgwood, the
youngest son of the potter, and his friend Humphry
Davy. In principle, its origins go back much farther

than that. Certainly, the experiments of Johann Schulze about 1725, with the discoloration of photo-sensitive mixtures of silver salts by exposing them to light through stencils in which words were cut, are to be considered significant as precursors in the development of direct contact photo-methods if not in the photographic process itself. With little doubt, in more remote ages, textile designers, for instance, were aware of the manner in which sunlight dis-coloured certain dyed fabrics, leaving imprinted on them the patterns of objects which by their super-imposition had inhibited the action of the solar rays.

Talbot's first advertised photographic process was called 'photogenic drawing'; in principle it was not different from that of Schulze. Photogenic drawing paper was first offered for sale in the spring of 1839 and with it, as one advertisement

Corot: Landscape sketch
Cliché-verre 1855

49

suggested, 'the most delicate and beautiful object either of nature or art may be accurately copied'. By contact printing Talbot reproduced a number of plant and lace forms, a few of which still survive. In a letter that year he wrote, 'nothing [is] more perfect . . . than the images of leaves and flowers that one can get with the July sunlight, the light penetrating through the leaves draws every vein of them'. Though in the faded remains of Talbot's photogenic pictures little sign of such veinous structures can be detected we may assume that originally – especially if the greater translucency of dried foliated forms was utilized – the delicate webbing of leaves in addition to the flat contoured shapes was recorded. Another application of photography without the use of the camera was that known as the *cliché verre*. And though its name suggests an origin in France it appears first to have been practised in England. Generically it is similar to some of the photographs produced probably by Wedgwood and Davy, by Nicéphore Niepce in the 1820s and by Talbot: the superimposition of an image through which light may pass in varying degrees will record that image on a prepared ground. Some of the earliest surviving photographs were made by waxing or oiling drawings and engravings to make them translucent before using them as 'negatives'. Immediately after Talbot's process was announced a small group of artists in London proposed their own methods for drawing and painting on glass to be used for making direct photographic prints. The engravers Frederick Havell and James Willmore described two fairly simple means for producing these pictures, which they said the sun may print and multiply with perfect identity forever. The first required that a glass plate be covered with a smoked etching ground and the design scratched through. In the second the picture was painted on the glass with a semi-opaque varnish, the thickness carefully controlled to produce the

necessary photographic tone. The use of the term
cliché verre, it seems, coincides with the period in the
early 1850s when the Barbizon painters, Corot,
Daubigny, Millet and others in the Fontainebleau
forest and Delacroix in Paris, enthusiastically applied
themselves to the technique. From the appearance

of their prints, one of the advantages of the *cliché
verre* was in the extraordinary flow of line obtainable
on the hard slick surfaces of glass plates. As a method
for reproduction it might then have equalled that
of engraving, for example, were it not for the stigma

already attached to the photographic process in relation to art. Later in England George Cruikshank employed this 'etching on glass' method which was then used, not directly to produce photographs as had the French artists, but as a negative with which to photograph onto a prepared zinc plate, in its turn etched and used for printing. Several years ago suggestions were made elaborating on the *cliché verre* technique. The skilful application of design on glass plates which are then used as negatives has been little explored in the field of graphic arts. The use of mutually repellent substances such as glycerine and ink will, it is said, produce interesting visual effects. The variations obviously are unlimited.

The photogenic drawing method never really went out of favour. From the period of its first popular application to the modern use of a similar but slightly more involved technique by the artists Christian Schad, Man Ray, Tristan Tzara and Moholy-Nagy one can find in modest little notices scattered about the pages of photographic journals, references to direct contact techniques without the use of the ordinary type of negative. For those, as one reads, who are frightened by the bewildering array of photographic paraphernalia, who are repelled by the stinks and stains of photo-chemicals, photography without a camera, the image fixed simply and quickly, had a great appeal. A large number of so-called 'printing out papers' of many types and colours was available. Of these, the cheapest and most convenient probably was ferro-prussiate or blue-print paper which after exposure requires only washing in water. Several variations of photogenic drawing, in which the image either was formed directly or was latent and had to be developed, were proposed in the nineteenth century, among them the superimposition of forms and sometimes the combination of a vignette with a proper negative, by which those quaint portraits emerging from a leaf or shell were obtained.

Heft 50   *1920*   Preis 2 Mark

DIE·WOCHE

MON   HRIFT

Druck und Verlag von August Scherl G.m.b.H., Berlin SW

Warenzeichen Nr. 5029

Though traditionally relegated to the more menial manipulatory techniques such as vignetting and fogging, or classified as a kind of sub-art as in the case of direct leaf and pattern prints, soon after the appearance of Cubism and abstract art, photography without the use of a camera took on a new importance. Just as the needs of photographers influenced by Impressionist painting had been somewhat satisfied by the gum-bichromate process, so were new techniques like Coburn's capable of conveying in visual terms the photographic counterparts to current aesthetic notions. What had been called photogenic drawing and, consistent with contemporary styles in art, had more or less reproduced the natural appearances of objects, was now in the 'modern era' employed to distort them. Perhaps the

Man Ray: *Rayographs 1921–25 Courtesy the artist*

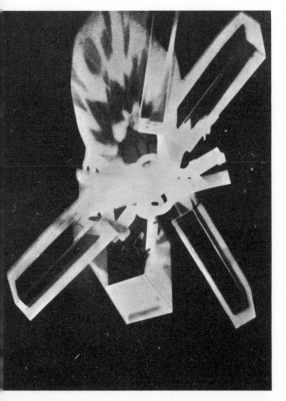

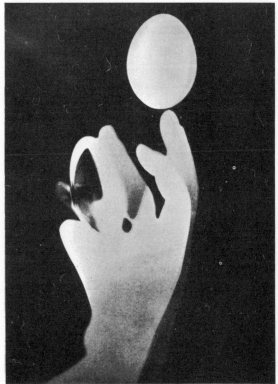

first photographs of this kind in our century, dating from 1918, were those of Christian Schad, a member of the anti-art Dada group in Zurich. These the artist called 'Schadographs' and as in Talbot's and others' leaf and lace forms were made by arranging a Schwitters-like collage of opaque and translucent paper cuttings and other peripherally identifiable objects on photo-sensitive paper, exposing and developing the image which might then be enhanced by the addition of drawing or painting. In 1921, elaborating this technique, Man Ray, an artist connected with the Dada group in Paris, produced his first 'Rayographs'. By utilizing both flat and three-dimensional objects he was able to induce sensations of indefinable floating forms in an illimitable space – something practically unattainable with previous methods. Also in the '20s Man Ray introduced an interesting photographic aberration called solarization – known since the 1860s as the Sabattier effect – into the repertory of the creative photographer. This technique by which a curious and evocative linear effect is coupled with a photographic tonality was later heavily exploited by photographers, often very successfully.

In his recent book, *Self Portrait*, Ray writes of chancing upon the Rayograph process when as an impecunious fashion photographer in Paris he was forced to make contact prints due to the lack of proper photographic equipment: 'One sheet of photo paper got into the developing tray – a sheet unexposed that had been mixed with those already exposed under the negatives . . . and as I waited in vain a couple of minutes for an image to appear, regretting the waste of paper, I mechanically placed a small glass funnel, the graduate and the thermometer in the tray on the wetted paper. I turned on the light; before my eyes an image began to form, not quite a simple silhouette of the objects as in a straight photograph, but distorted and refracted by the glass more or less in contact with the paper and

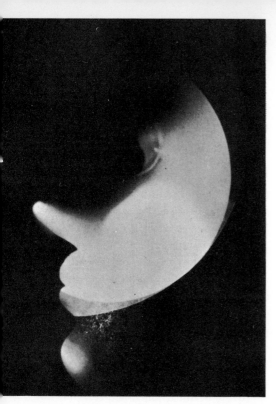

Moholy-Nagy: *Photogram* 1926
Permission Klinkhardt and Biermann, Brunswick

standing out against a black background, the part directly exposed to light. I remembered when I was a boy, placing fern leaves in a printing frame with proof paper, exposing it to sunlight, and obtaining a white negative of the leaves.' Ray then made more prints in this manner, but first placing objects on dry paper. The next day Tristan Tzara saw the results pinned onto the wall and proclaimed them pure Dada creations. Tzara favourably compared the Rayographs with what he considered inferior flat textural prints made a few years earlier by Schad, and that night was spent by both Ray and Tzara making more of these new kinds of photographs.

Ray was an exponent of the opinion so obstreperously advocated in the first few decades of this century, that in a work of art both the subject and the medium must be transformed. The addition of extraneous material to the picture was now considered an advantage; indeed anything was permitted so long as the essential thought of feeling was communicated: 'Whether a painter, emphasizing the importance of the idea he wishes to convey, introduces bits of ready-made chromos alongside

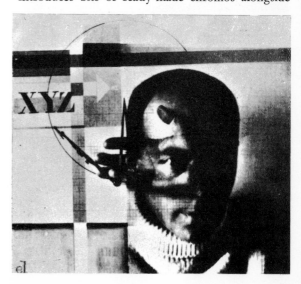

El Lissitzky: *Typophoto*. Mixed techniques *c* 1929

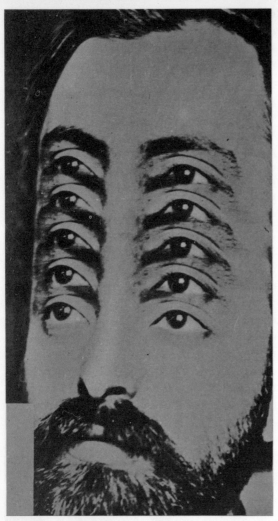

Keystone Views: *The Eye-tree*
By superimposition 1925
Permission Keystone Press Agency Ltd

his handiwork, or whether another, working direct
ly with light and chemistry, so deforms the subjec
as almost to hide the identity of the original, an
creates a new form, the ensuing violation of th
medium employed is the most perfect assurance o
the author's convictions. A certain amount of con
tempt for the material employed to express an ide
is indispensable to the purest realization of this idea

Evolving the photo-techniques employed by Ma
Ray, the artist Laszlo Moholy-Nagy devoted him
self to what he would have thought of as objectiv
but which was later to be called subjective, photo
graphy. His photograms appear first in 1922, onl
a year after those of Ray, but Moholy's conceptio
of the scope of the photographic medium differe
from that of his predecessor. He explored it
physical properties and visual applications wit
great assiduity, and he formulated a startling philo
sophical idea about 'the new vision' in which th
photographic image played an important symboli
role. He later wrote of an earlier desire to divest hi
art of the personal touch and to achieve machine
like perfection. He gave up signing his paintings
putting numbers, letters and other data on the back
of his work as if they were cars, airplanes, or othe
industrial products. He utilized the airbrush and th
spraygun to produce surfaces devoid of signs c
individual treatment – to go beyond vanity, as h
stated, into the realm of objective validity. It wa
with this calculated anonymity that Moholy pro
duced his photographs, and especially his photo
grams. To him the camera, or the photographi
process in general, was a means of reducing th
gap between art and the non-art of industrial pro
duction. Thus his photographs were produced no
as art forms, but as technical demonstrations c
objects recording their own spatial relations b
light. The extremism of Moholy's concept is illus
trated by his description of a method he used i

Double-exposed portrait of Hannah Höch *c* 1925

composing, in 1922, five paintings in porcelain enamel. It was done entirely by telephone. In this way the artist, or more correctly the designer, using sets of standardized colours and sheets of regulation graph paper, communicated all the necessary information to a factory manager at the other end of the line.

These attitudes were formulated probably during Moholy's association as a professor with the Weimar Bauhaus from 1923, and derived largely from the theories of the Russians Malevich, Rodchenko and Lissitzky, the last two pioneers in the development of photomontage and the introduction of photography into typographical design. Paralleling Rodchenko's new photography appearing in the Constructivist journals, *Left* and *New Left*, in 1925 the Bauhaus produced the book *Painting, Photography, Film* which contained a large number of highly imaginative photographs by Laszlo and Lucia Moholy-Nagy, by Man Ray, Hannah Höch, Paul Citroën and others; photograms, photomontages, double-exposures, negative prints, low-angled shots were among them. This perhaps was the first time that a collection of works in photography was published in which most of the traditional rules governing creative photography were ignored, and one has only to consult the current issues of established photographic periodicals to gauge the extent of the change which this implies.

In 1925 the Bauhaus removed to Dessau and there Moholy-Nagy was instrumental in establishing photography as an essential part of the programme. Several other artists were associated with this group; among them Herbert Bayer, Georg Muche, Lux Feininger, Joost Schmidt, and Xanti Schawinsky had already produced photographs of outstanding merit or had incorporated photography into their graphic work following the techniques of the Russians, thus laying the foundations for the photographic workshop which came into being in 1929.

Walter Gropius, the director of the Bauhaus
called Moholy's *The New Vision* (first published in
1928) 'A standard grammar of modern design'. It
was in fact a detailed prospectus for the course of
studies, and in it photography was given a significant position. Believing themselves on the threshold
of the future, Moholy and his associates were particularly interested in a modern conception of space
composition; a new counterpoint of space, Gropius
called it: the fourth dimensional element of time
simultaneity, recorded by light. With a kind of
revolutionary fervour they viewed their activities as
a counterpart of the great social and political up-
heaval so immanent in that time. The Bauhaus
programme was pre-eminently a humanitarian one
with the ultimate purpose of utilizing the machine
and other techniques for the advantage of all; to
recover the 'biological bases of human life', to
satisfy essential rhythms, to make life fuller and less
hysterical. Thus photography became on the one
hand a technique, purely and simply, to convey
information, to record all Bauhaus activities, to
record space and time by light, and on the other
primarily in form of montage, an expressive tool.
In 1937 when Moholy transplanted the Bauhaus to
Chicago's Institute of Design, there too photography played a prominent part in the obligatory
foundation course. The Light workshop covered
photography and the motion picture, light display
and advertising art. 'Photography', Moholy wrote
'is included in the preliminary course; being itself
a perfect instrument of exact representation it serves
as a means of comparison for the quality of manual
craftsmanship. The illiterate of the future will be,
we believe, the person who cannot photograph.'

Despite Moholy's determination to eradicate all
semblances of individualism and style from the
photographs produced in his workshops, despite
the punctilious laboratory vernacular with which
those photographs were described, time and tradi-

tion have demonstrated how dated, how stylish and
how expressive such products of the Bauhaus were.
Photograms were there conceived more as technical
experiments than poetic emanations: 'light painting,'
it was called, 'photographic surface treatment by
light', and typically, 'this is the recording of light
as it hit a projection screen – in this case, the sensitive layer of the photographic paper'. Moholy's
desire to create a new and impersonal visual
concept of space directly from light presupposed the
use of the photogram to record kinetic light and
shadow effects, reflections, mirrorings and any
other phenomena which would increase the scope
of the study of new space relationships. His belief
that Cubism utilized photography in its study of

surface values is probably without foundation, but it may have influenced the way in which Moholy conceived of a new kind of photographic image based on Cubist forms.

Among the many different types of photographs which illustrated various editions of *The New Vision* and which undoubtedly were of major influence on later photographers and artists, were photo-micrographs to demonstrate the structure of materials, aerial photographs showing unexpected terrestrial patterns, photographic recordings of acoustical phenomena, time exposures of city scenes at night – called light diagrams – in which the paths of movement of lighted objects record the interpenetrations of forms, so-called light projectors and modulators, and superimposed images which create ambiguous spatial relations of form – not unlike Cubist pictures.

In 1929, coinciding with the beginning of its formal course in photography, the Bauhaus co-operated in staging a large exhibition of photography in Stuttgart which, probably for the first time on such a scale, presented a number of new and undoubtedly startling kinds of photographic images. In the same year, Franz Roh, one of the leading spokesmen in Germany for the new photography, published – also in Stuttgart – *foto-auge*. Assisted by the organizers of the *Film und Foto* exhibition, Roh and his associate, the typographer Jan Tschichold, compiled more than seventy works from several countries which together formed a new catalogue of *avant-garde* photography. Roh argued, as did some of his nineteenth century predecessors, that too great a technical knowledge, or (more precisely) too much of an infatuation with it, was likely to become an inhibiting factor in the production of photographs claiming expressive merit. Often, he stated, amateurs whose work may be technically lacking bring to this medium a rejuvenescence unknown to the

Moholy-Nagy: *The Shattered Marriage* 1925
Permission Klinkhardt and Biermann, Brunswick

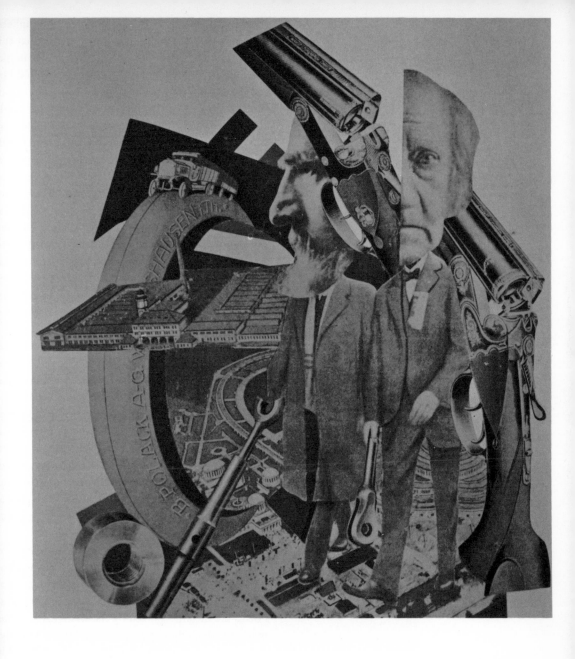

Hannah Höch: *The Millionaire c* 1925

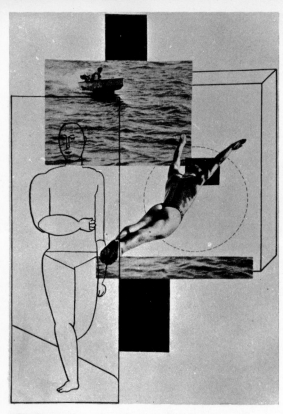

Willi Baumeister: Combination photographs and drawing *c* 1929

more conventional professional photographers Echoing Bauhaus socialism, Roh believed that this is possible by virtue of the happy fact that, unlike previous graphic techniques, photography could be handled by all. And it is significant that from beginning to end his book does not contain a single capital letter: 'to maintain that "short cuts" by relieving him of all effort, lead to man's greater dullness and laziness, is romanticism' and 'it was likewise romanticism to assert that everyone who has something to say will find a way of saying it, only when the technical media have become so simple that everybody can learn to apply them, will they become a keyboard for the expression of many.' He was enthusiastic about the liberating effects of the camera in much the same manner as those nineteenth-century scientists who saw and applauded in the machine the end of all deprivations previously suffered by the masses.

Those who reject the kind of photographs reproduced in his book, exclaimed Roh, are the same people who refuse new painting and new graphic art whether it be abstract, constructivist, or objectivist art – the last presumably referring to the new Magic Realist movement which he supported. These photographs do not express only the beauty of the world but also its excitement, its cruelty and its strangeness. He divides applied photography into five categories: the photogram, the reality-photo, photomontage, photo with etching or painting, and photographs in connection with typography.

In contrast to the technological determinism of Moholy-Nagy, Roh muses poetically over the photogram. It hovers excitingly between abstract geometrical tracery and the echo of objects, he writes. Forms are metamorphized by the strange, luminous world in which they appear to exist. Unlike Moholy Roh does not find any suggestions of a calculable space in photograms. He sees instead a wonderful ambiguity of transparent shapes which intersect in a

Max Ernst: Surrealist photomontage.
ainting and photographs *c* 1929

vast cosmos of myriad shades of grey. It is this polyphony of tones, as he calls it, which gives photography such sublime possibilities.

Of the reality-photo, what we now call straight photography, Roh first describes the use of new subject matter such as sewage canals or any other 'fragments of reality', however commonplace, which can be made expressive and symbolic. The old is seen anew, he proclaims, and contrary to the Impressionist twilight in which photographers had immersed their subjects, 'today everything is brought out clearly'. New optical attractions in the form of ingeniously conceived scale, perspective, view-point and camera angle, and new valuation given to the inverse image of the negative print, is discussed. The utilization of these and other pictorial techniques could bring photography to an audacious but more elevated plane than ever before.

This irrepressible spokesman for creative photography praises the marvellous works of Max Ernst

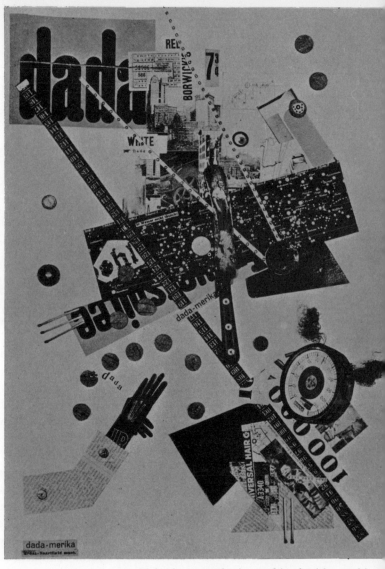

George Grosz and John Heartfield:
dada-merika. Typophoto *c* 1929

in which photography is combined with graphic o
painting techniques. 'To maintain that here is
mingling of heterogeneous elements that can neve
combine is but an empty doctrine.'

The conception of the photomontage he attri
butes to the Futurist and Dada artists and thoug
formerly it resulted in the demolition of form, i

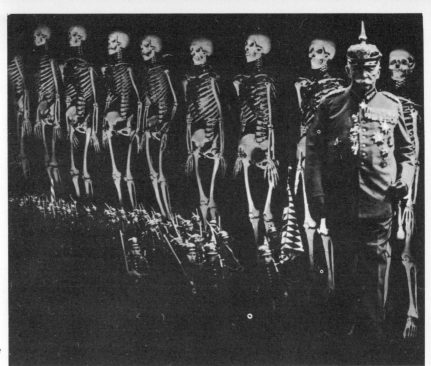

John Heartfield:
After Twenty Years.
Photomontage 1934
*Permission Deutsche Akademie
der Kunst, Berlin*

a chaotic whirl, it has now been rectified, Roh assures his readers, systematically constructed and with an almost classic moderation and calm. Montage is based on 'a deep need of human imagination'. Many of those delightful scrap albums periodically found in old book shops, in which the fancy is indulged in bizarre and enchanting combinations of images and materials, confirm his belief. Outstanding in the effective use of the photomontage technique were the artists George Grosz and John Heartfield. The latter's brilliant photographic excoriations of Prussian militarism, monopoly capitalism and of the Nazi regime have perhaps never yet been equalled. Grosz wrote to Roh: 'Yes! you are right, Heartfield and I had already in 1915 made interesting photopasting-montage-experiments'. The painter's portrait of his friend, *The Montage-Paster Heartfield* (1920) is probably a comment on the sub-

John Heartfield: *The Cabbage Head: Away with the Blindfolds.* Photomontage 193⬚
Permission Deutsche Akademie der Kunst, Berlin

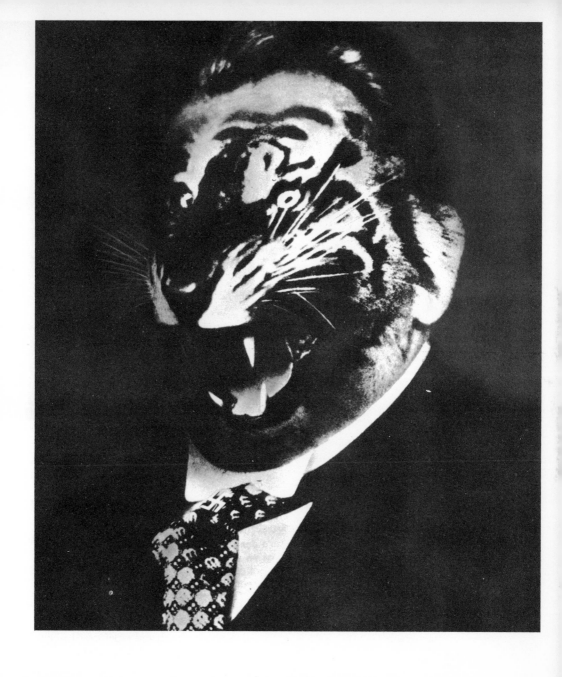

John Heartfield: Photomontage 1931 *Permission Deutsche Akademie der Kunst, Berlin*

George Grosz: *The Montage-paster Heartfield*
Combination painting and photographs 1920

ject's devotion to his chosen medium. The photo
graph of some mechanical assembly is mounte
over the area of the heart. Also in 1915 Carlo Carr:
one of the Italian Futurists, produced a strang
painting of what appears to be a nude figure upo
which was pasted a piece of a photograph represen
ing a military subject: the title: 'French Offici:
Observing Enemy Movements'. Roh saw that fro:
fragments of reality a more complex structure coul
be created, and photomontage and the combinatio
of the photograph and typeforms he believed woul
in the future be used in pictorial humour, in comme:
cial advertising, on book jackets and to produc
pictures significant in themselves.

Carlo Carrà: *French Official Observing Enemy Movements*
1915 *Courtesy Il Milione, Milan*

The magical persuasive power of the photographic image is no less germane to twentieth-century techniques such as multiple-exposure and montage than it was to that which produced a murderer in the eye of a dead man or effected a material communion with the spiritual world. The irrational juxtapositions to be found in the photomontages, as well as in other works, of the Dada and Surrealist artists are the more startling because some of their components convey a believable segment of the natural world. The monstrous fabrications of subject, the impossible scale and space and other features in such art, which are entirely contradictory to the laws of physical nature, somehow appear plausible – perhaps even more so than do similar forms in drawing and painting – when they are symbolically keyed with scraps of logic in the form, say, of photographs.

Most of the photographs presented in *foto-auge* appear surprisingly new even today. Almost all of the pictorial techniques described by Roh are here explored, and several of the works included are by artists better known as painters and designers than as photographers: Max Ernst, George Grosz, El Lissitzky, Willi Baumeister. Bizarre natural patterns revealed by the aerial photograph, the ghostly botanical forms of a negative X-ray print, another intriguing X-ray photograph of the contents of a beaded handbag, photogram fantasies of light and shadow, startling surrealist photo-paintings in which the photographic fragments in a new context assume a shrill intensity, combination pictures in which photographs, prints, typographical forms and drawings are merged to form potent new images, are all abundant visual evidence supporting Roh's claims for the new photography.

The following year Roh published *L. Moholy-Nagy, 60 Fotos* in which the author expounds the new conception of photography. Though photography is above all the technique of reporting, and though certain theoreticians protest against the more liberal

Georges Hugnet: Surrealist photomontage *c* 1936

Moholy-Nagy: *How to Remain Young and Beautiful*. Negative print of photomontage 1925
Permission Klinkhardt and Biermann, Brunswick

conception of photography as an end in itself, the process lends itself to manipulation, to forming (as he calls it). Not only does the choice of object or viewpoint, of perspective effect, light, composition, focus, of the photographic materials themselves, offer a vast scale of freedom with which to interpret the object, but as in the unorthodox work of Moholy, the negative print and his photograms, for example, are merely other means of dealing with light, which will yet give rise to new forms. Roh argues the priority of photograms: the photogram is as old as the photograph, but credit is due to Man Ray and Moholy for applying it in modern form. In photomontage Moholy, he says, belongs to the pioneers and though this technique dates back to some generations ago (see H. P. Robinson and 'combination printing'), it yet has only in the present become a deliberately forming process. Roh followed in that year with another book on the sixty photographs of Aenne Biermann whose work, not as far-ranging as that of Moholy, was restricted to the imaginative use of the camera: close-ups, pattern shots, negative prints, reflections and unusual angles of vision, unexpected compositions. In the introduction he continues the arguments propounded in the first book: photography as a mechanism of mere reproduction kills the creative in us, and becomes a menace to art. As to the proposition that photography was not an art, 'that depends only on how the concept art is defined. If under art only purely manual production is understood, a new category can be established for photography. But if, on the other hand, art is understood to be nothing else but fully expressive, self-purposed form called forth by man, good photographs must be included.'

The interest in books describing the novel and curious effects of photographic experiments may be estimated by the fact that Woodbury's *Photographic Amusements* appeared between 1896 and 1937 in

ving Browning: 'Bas-relief' photograph *c* 1937
rmission Amphoto, New York

eleven editions. With the publication in 1939 of
Andreas Feininger's *New Paths in Photography* the
spirit of the Bauhaus and the ideas of Franz Roh
were given fresh impetus. Now several new kinds
of images and variations on earlier ones – many of
which previously would have been excused or dis-

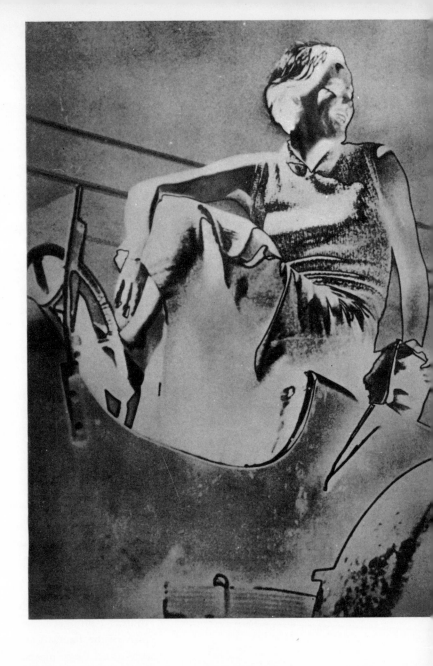

Andreas Feininger: Print from solarized positive transparency *c* 1939
Permission Amphoto, New York

Andreas Feininger: A Gothic portal. Print from solarized negative transparency
c 1939 *Permission Amphoto, New York*

missed as photographic deviations – were seriously proposed as an essential part of the vocabulary of the creative photographer: 'a thorough understanding of the means photography has to offer' is fundamental in its development as a graphic art. His own photographs are reproduced: a splendid display of creative techniques which include negative prints, positive and negative solarized and relief images, reticulated (granulated) ones and many permutations of these. The author of this admirable book, however, seems to echo the traditional extra-sensitivity of photographers in their relation to painting: 'the mistake is still made of mixing up photography and painting'; other than the creative urge the two have 'nothing in common'. Reacting perhaps against what might easily have been considered the excessive use of ready-made photographs or of the photogram by Surrealist, Magic Realist and other artists, Feininger writes we begin to feel more and more the need to regain a feeling for material, to come into contact with reality instead of artifices.

In the past two decades, aware that no photographer – however mean his talents – would consider himself anything other than creative and that the term itself had largely been usurped by those who believed in it least, several writers have attempted to give back the word its essential meaning. Some perceptive observations about photography as an art were, for example, published in 1943 by the photographer Phillip Andrews who believed that as part of his training a photographer should acquaint himself with, or even duplicate, the experiments of early pioneers just as a doctor studies the crude experiments of Pasteur, Newton and Faraday. Writing of the rarity of photograms, for instance, in exhibitions and in photographic periodicals, Andrews finds the cause in the antipathy of most photographers to anything which does not conform precisely to the academic concepts

Pierre Boucher: Series of six variations of positive and negative images and displacement effects *c* 1939

Larry Rivers: Announcement for exhibition of his paintings 1964. *Courtesy the artist*

of photography... photography as a form of artistic expression is lamentably far behind photography as a purely technical development. The belief that photography has no relation to any other art form, he continues, has probably, and justifiably, grown out of abortive attempts to simulate the *superficial* technique of painting rather than its intrinsic qualities. More recently, exponents of subjective photography – like their spiritual counterparts in the last century – agree that one of the major impediments to creative photography is the obtuseness of critics whose outstanding qualification is the knowledge of the *technique* of photography.

Yet today there are many signs indicating that we are on the verge of a new period in the creative use of photography. *L'Année Dernière à Marienbad*, in the cinema, exemplifies this. The merging of diverse photographic procedures with other graphic means seems to increase as the tentative visual essays usually associated with such a combination diminish. In painting and drawing, notably in the work of R.B. Kitaj and Robert Rauschenberg, photographic images – like Roh's fragments of reality – are transformed in their fusion with the other elements of the pictures. A few artists have put into their service the very fabric of the photo-reproductive processes, and Muybridge emerges in the form of the Polyfoto. The expressive possibilities of the numerous new photo-copying machines which have been flooding the market are gradually being explored. Some artists have recently produced bizarre and exquisite images by a system of cumulative projections and by metamorphical progressions from the photographic to the graphic form. And in essence many early photographic techniques are being revived and effectively translated into contemporary terms. More schools of art are beginning to think seriously of photography as having an important function in their programmes. In addi-

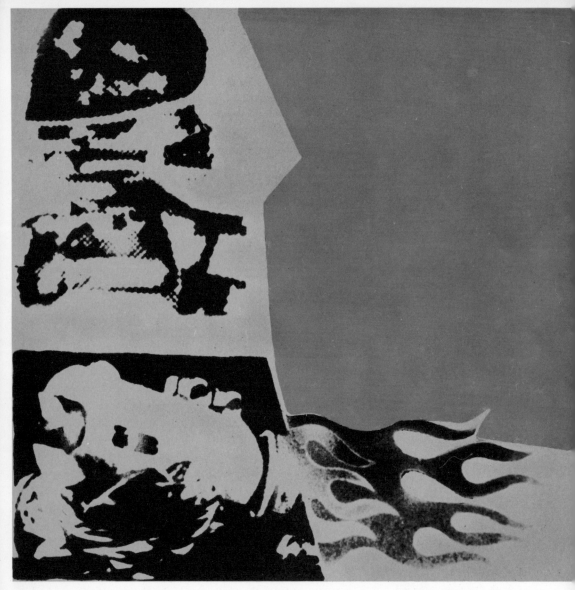

Gerald Laing: *Vehicle*. Photo-silkscreen and stencil on silver foil 1964 *Courtesy the artist. Photo: Sally Burgess*

Robert Rauschenberg: *Tracer* 1964 Oil on canvas
Collection Mr and Mrs Frank Titelman, Altoona, Pa.
Courtesy Leo Castelli, New York. Photo: Rudy Burckhard

Ken Randall: Painted cliché-verre 1963
Courtesy the artist

tion to its usefulness as a recording mechanism its meaning for other creative work is becoming apparent. In itself immensely capable of artistic expression the photograph may furthermore convey unknown aspects of nature to the inquisitive eye and stimulate works of art in other media. And it may function directly in the fabrication of some assemblage of pictorial forms.

The traditional difficulty of balancing the mechanical with the imaginative use of photography still operates. In schools of photography meaningful art education is often lacking and on the strength of their technical abilities alone students, deprived of a richer artistic training, are sent forth inculcated with the belief that they are creative photographers and artists. It is yet a fact that today, as in the past, the most inspiring and provocative works in photography come as much (and probably more) from those who are in the first place artists.

In our time it seems entirely appropriate that the widest choice be open to artists. Those using the camera or other photographic means to produce works of artistic merit should seek to exploit their medium in the most adventurous ways. Soon enough the aesthetic myopia which so often accompanies either too intense or too insufficient a belief in one's own work may cause a temporary or even permanent blindness. The derogatory use of the term artifice is more often than not a bugaboo. Art *is* artifice. Its reality is of another nature than that of the purely physical world. For many working with the photographic medium the term photographer is itself superfluous, just as are painter and sculptor as little applicable to those for whom all means and all materials may be used to express some artistic idea. Often art is treated as though it were politics and it appears grossly inconsistent with an understanding of what has happened during the past hundred years to continue to indulge in the narrow classifications of artistic validity.

Intelligently imposed restrictions, purposeful limitations, which periodically an artist may place on himself can obviously be beneficial. But surely such limitations are futile if in fact they are only circumventions. One need not make oneself blind to enhance one's hearing. Since Pliny at least we have been reminded of the virtues inherent in the limitation of one's means. Pliny insisted that Apelles and other Greek painters had advantageously confined themselves to a palette of four colours only; this being an example, if not a cause, of their

Illustrations overleaf:
Gerry Jones:
Painted photograph using paper negative 1963
courtesy the artist

D. Holden and R. Hyde: Projected image on nude 1963

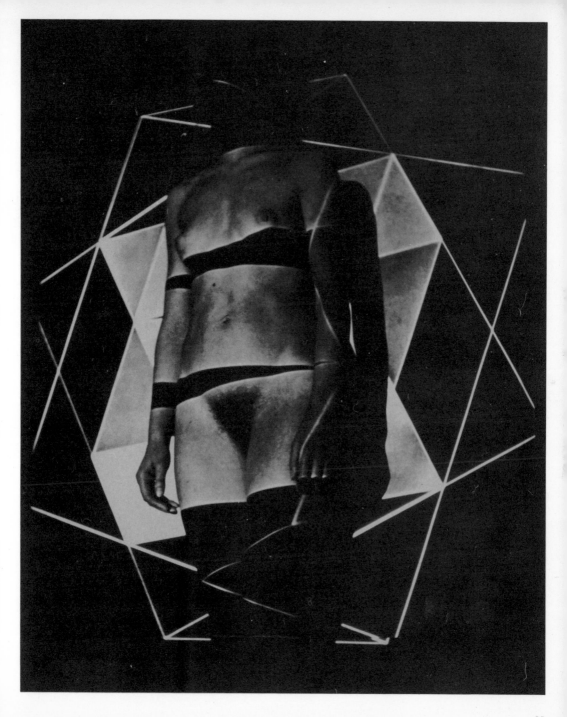

Geoffrey Ireland: Photo-drawing 1956
Courtesy the artist

Geoffrey Ireland: Photographed design on plate usin
crystalline solution 1955
Courtesy the artist

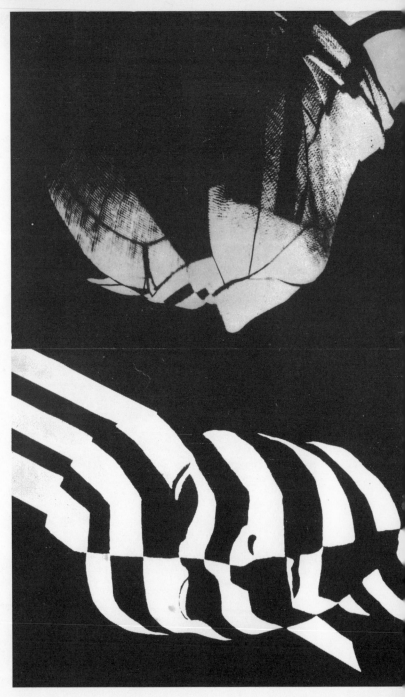

Robert Hyde and Peter Jones:
Mixed techniques 1964
Courtesy the artists

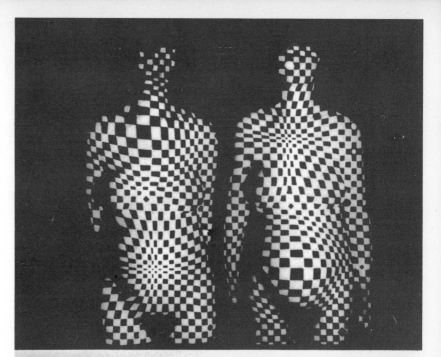

greatness. Whatever Apelles may or may not hav
done, it is nevertheless a fact that many artists in a
media have in the past and in the present profite
also by taking a permissive rather than a restrictiv
attitude to those media.

Many of the examples which have been discusse
and illustrated here are not necessarily put forwar
as outstanding works of photographic art. The
may even be trivial; some of them are. But howeve
one may value them, they have been chosen becau
each of them is believed to embody some essenti
idea, some potent promise which, put in the wa
of the creative artist may, like the commonpla
exteriors of crystalliferous cavities, yield unsuspec
ed gems. The merits of so-called straight phot
graphy or of any other kind of photograph
naturalism should not be ignored or minimize
Indeed it would be superfluous to elaborate on th
excellence of a prodigious number of photograph
of this kind produced especially in the 1940's ar
50's following one stream of Bauhaus photograph
But because of the paucity of literature which trea
photographic unorthodoxy in a serious way, ar
because books and magazine articles on creativ
photography at best show only limited interest in
exaggeration was considered necessary. Intrinsi
ally all images, however innocuous or incongruo
they may appear, have an aesthetic potential. Mar
of those produced by some photographic mear
and which artistic propriety found untenable,
which were proposed with the self-deprecatory ir
plications that they were only accidents, tricks
amusements, provided imaginative photographe
and painters as well, with both the visual confirm
tions of their most daring ideas and the inspiratio
to carry them out.